KICK THE BABY
OFF THE CLIFF

It Looks Innocent, But It's Not!

by
Karen Wourms

W0010498

DEDICATION

I want to thank my husband, Mike. Without his expertise and his willing heart to give me the time and loving attention this project needed, I would never have been able to start it or complete it without him. He has been my biggest cheerleader; his love for me was evident through his hard work and diligence.

I also dedicate this book to my three supportive sons, Paul, Tim and Mitch, and to their beautiful wives, Janet, Terri and Raquel, and to my wonderful grandbabies, Austin, Tanner and Valerie. All of you earnestly reflect the godly self-talk I am so blessed to receive, and that I write about in this book.

TABLE OF CONTENTS

v

FOREWORD
BY
BEV SMITH

My parents schooled me early in the fine art of reading, and today I constantly devour books as a talk show host; I've probably read and own over 3,000 books in my lifetime (not counting newspapers and magazine articles). But when I received Karen's book for review, it somehow stood apart from the others. The first thing that struck me was her shocking title – *Kick the Baby Off the Cliff.*

"Is this a book on child abuse?" I wondered. As I began to read, I realized it wasn't. Instead, Karen writes about the destructive messages we send ourselves every day, and then tells us how to change them into what she calls 'godly thoughts' that lead to creative and joyful living.

There are countless instances in my own life where I have been the victim of destructive messages which robbed me of my power over my circumstances. As I read further, I identified place after place where I could have avoided so many unpleasant messes had I known then how to 'start kickin'."

"Oprah has a successful show, and if I were as good as Oprah, I'd be rich and popular too."

"Kick that baby, girl. God is using your talk show to impact your city and the nation. Be grateful for the forum and platform He has given you."

Here's an amazing truth! When we speak to others, we easily encourage them that they DO have the power to change, but when it comes to ourselves, deep down inside we aren't so sure we can change. We're like the shoemaker whose kids are walking barefoot.

Don't be fooled by the baby's innocent looks! This baby is dangerous...you MUST kick that baby off the cliff! You can because you can do all things through Christ who strengthens you (Philippians 4:13).

CIRCUMSTANCES ARE CONSTANT

The challenges never go away. Currently, my daddy is struggling with serious illness, my knee hurts constantly (and my insurance will not cover the shots I need), my finances sometimes are a struggle...so it is easy to listen to that baby. He has flashing lights and even does visuals. But in the midst of my challenges, when my blood pressure is elevated, as I try to deal with the grief and anger of watching my father fade away, and when I start to moan and groan about my circumstances, I now hear a small voice saying, *"Kick the baby off the cliff."*

"But Lord, why me? Where's my angel to watch over me? Are You really there for me in the midst of these things?"

"Of course I am. Kick the baby off the cliff."

When someone tells me, "Girl, you really look great," my baby replies, "Oh come on! Can't you see I'm wearing a girdle! I can't wait to get home to take this thing off and breathe." Karen's book teaches the inner truth (how God sees me); I am learning to let the voice of God be the one I hear.

Speak God's Words. Friend, as hard as you work on your job, you need to work harder on your life and thoughts. For those of us who are life-coaches (we were once called motivational speakers), our message should be that there's no end to the boundless creativity in you. You don't need to have a better figure or a rich uncle...you need to erase your old tapes and replace them with God's Words and God's heart for your life.

A RECIPE FOR LIFE!

The average restaurant is launched because the owner (cook) created some wonderful recipes. Karen's book teaches how to create and savor the wonderful thoughts in our lives that line up with God's Word...words that give us the power to change our attitudes and our old, destructive self talk.

We remember mottos like "See the USA in your Chevrolet." I pray that Karen's book becomes a life-time motto for all of us. Whenever ungodly self talk tries to enter our lives, I pray we all learn to "Kick the baby off the cliff." It is not what we eat that harms us, it is what we say that messes with our minds. It is what we think about who we are as human beings that matters.

Personally, Karen's book gave me permission to talk about my own victories and failings in my book, *A Funny Thing Happened on the Way to Success*. I believe her honesty helped me to be open and real with my own story, hopefully helping others to change their lives.

I may never be a size seven again, but that doesn't mean I go around the rest of my life saying, "I am not good enough." I once avoided parties and major events because of how the fat I carried made me feel. Karen is saying, "Kick that baby." Challenge destructive messages. Don't give them sanction.

"But Bev, it's a baby."

"It's not what it seems. It looks innocent, but it's not."

As for me, I'm going to keep on kickin' that baby for the rest of my life, even with my bad knee.

Thank you, Karen.

Bev Smith
Nationally Syndicated Talk Show Host

INTRODUCTION

May God Grant You Good Kickin'

For the last fifteen years I have taught a class with my friend, Margo, called *"Women With Childhood Abuse Healing Workshop,"* and, I have had the joy of teaching a course called *"Marriage God's Way"* with my husband, Mike. In both classes, I would always take one session to teach on the subject of godly and ungodly self-talk. Invariably, after I had taught on that little-understood subject, a number of people would come up to me, asking, "Karen, do you have any written material on your self-talk lesson that I can take home with me?"

Through the years it has become apparent that the impact of those simple spiritual principles God has given me on self-talk profoundly touched those who heard these biblical truths.

So, in a way I was already spiritually prepared when one day my husband, a Christian writer, said to me, "Honey, God's really put it on my heart to help you write a book on godly and ungodly self-talk." His sharing, and his willingness to help me write this book, pushed me into gear to put the real-life stories God has given me into *Kick the Baby Off the Cliff*.

The book you now hold in your hands has materialized as a simple matter of obedience to God's Holy Spirit, and because of the deep spiritual conviction that the biblical guidelines for godly self-talk have changed the lives of countless men and women who have applied these amazing spiritual principles.

Know this: God's principles will work for anyone, man, woman or child! The earlier you master and practice godly self-talk, the earlier the *"peace of God"* (Philippians 4:9) will start to flow in your life.

My prayer is that *Kick the Baby Off the Cliff* will help you understand and recognize a rather curious reality I have found in far too many Christian lives: the experience of personal futility in the midst of the salvation walk. One day the Holy Spirit placed these words in my heart, and they sum up what I mean by the futility/salvation experience:

A person can be saved, delivered from bondages, filled with the Holy Spirit, love and serve God, have a ministry...

AND STILL BE MISERABLE!

Why?

Because of ungodly self-talk.

This revelation gave me a sudden sense of understanding on how God wants to free many of His people through these spiritual principles. What I have come to call "ungodly self-talk" can undermine all the other powerful weapons God has given you for spiritual warfare and prosperous living, even destroying the power of your daily prayers!

When you learn how to *Kick the Baby Off the Cliff*, and eliminate ungodly self-talk from your life, you will begin to blossom into the fullness, wholeness and happiness God desires for you.

My prayer is that as you read this book of real-life stories, God will grant you good kickin'.

Karen Wourms

AN IMPORTANT NOTE
TO THE READER

My Dear Reader,

Please read the Scripture below – out loud – before you turn to Chapter One. It contains foundational, life-changing revelations from God's Word that are illustrated throughout the pages of *Kick the Baby Off the Cliff*. It is God's promise that as you recognize and adopt these truths, your life will never be the same again.

Karen Wourms

Then Jesus called to the crowd to come and hear.

"All of you listen," he said, "and try to understand. Your souls aren't harmed by what you eat, but by what you think and say!"

Then he went into a house to get away from the

crowds, and his disciples asked him what he meant by the statement he had just made.

"Don't you understand either?" he asked. "Can't you see that what you eat won't harm your soul? For food doesn't come in contact with your heart, but only passes through the digestive system." (By saying this he showed that every kind of food is kosher.)

And then he added, "<u>It is the thought-life that pollutes</u>. [My underline] For from within, out of men's hearts, come evil thoughts of lust, theft, murder, adultery, wanting what belongs to others, wickedness, deceit, lewdness, envy, slander, pride, and all other folly. <u>All these vile things come from within; they are what pollute you and make you unfit for God</u>." [My underline]

(Mark 7:14-23, The Living Bible)

# CHAPTER ONE

The Light and Dark Centers

During the eighteen months we lived in Louisiana in the late seventies, God answered my prayer for the perfect job: I was fortunate enough to work during the same hours when my children were in school. It really didn't matter to me what I did for work, but it was important to me that I could be home when my children were out of school. I wanted to be able to prepare their breakfast in the morning, and be there to greet them with snacks when they came home from school (yes, I'm Italian, and food is a vital part of my family heritage).

That dream job came to me through a learning center for adults who were mentally challenged. An organization hired me to work as an assistant in two of their centers – three days a week in the one across the Mississippi River (a ferry took my station wagon to the other side), and two days a week in the one on the Gramercy side of the river where we lived.

The experience of working at both centers taught me a valuable lesson: I witnessed firsthand how a loving teacher, or a not-so-loving teacher, could both produce "like kind" in their students.

THE DARK SIDE

On the far side of the river about fifteen students received instructions from two very negative teachers. Their commission was supposedly to train, help and encourage their students to produce something tangible that would be a source of pride. This center produced ceramics which were then sold to the public. The funds from the sale of these artifacts enabled the center staff to reward "the kids" (that's what I called these mentally challenged adults), by taking them out of the center for a day of play, traveling to the mall for lunch, or just going to a movie.

All day long, from 9 a.m. until 2 p.m., ceramics were the medium used to keep these kids busy. The center would make ceramic cows, turtles, horses, apples, alligators (it was Louisiana!) and many other cute curios. Since the two teachers in charge wanted their ceramic creations to be as close-to-perfection as possible..."award winning" was the way one put it – they allowed only one of the students in the class to actually scrape the ceramics since she could do it without breaking the pieces. Only two others were permitted to paint. The remaining students sat and talked most of the day; they were not allowed to work on the ceramics. Once in a great while they would be given the rare opportunity to sit with one tiny project in front of them to paint; that project would not be offered for sale.

The teachers frequently yelled at the class. In the entire time I was employed, I NEVER heard a single word of encouragement. Even lunchtime meals reflected discipline and seriousness.

I once heard one of the teachers say, "We are going to give them a party for Valentine's Day." When I enthusiastically asked, "What should I bring? What can I do to help?" She replied, "It really doesn't matter. They are all so stupid they wouldn't appreciate what you did anyway."

That pathetic attitude permeated the center across the river, so the kids became fearful of the teachers, and criticized each other. The center felt like a cold, unfriendly place; since the students had nothing else to do, and nowhere else to go, they unfortunately still came to the center.

A sense of seriousness permeated this group. They were afraid to do wrong, fearful of breaking anything, expecting to be criticized.

I hated working at this center!

Being one who enjoys laughter and fun, I determined to try and bring a little joy to the place. When one Christmas drew near, I decided to plan another party (Valentine's was a miserable bust). But when I suggested music for dancing, I was told, "You'll never get them to do anything. All they ever do is sit."

On the day of the Christmas party, the students sat at a long table with candy, a cupcake and a drink in front of them. Not much talking or laughing was going on. It didn't look like a party to me. The two teachers in charge were in another part of the room enjoying their own conversation, totally separated, emotionally and physically, from the kids.

Finally, I decided to put on a record while asking, "Who wants to dance with me?" At first, they all seemed very scared; no one volunteered. So, I went over to one of the shy students and took him by the hand and started dancing. Instantly, as if permission had suddenly been granted to be alive, the class started laughing, both from embarrassment and excitement, as though to say, "Hey, something different is going on here today. What is this? We've not experienced this here before."

After dancing and having a good time, displaying my silly steps and awkward twirls, laughter erupted from my dancing partner. Boldly, two girls stood up and started to join us.

Then two more.

Ultimately, almost all of the kids got up and danced, realizing that they didn't have to do anything special. No one was criticizing them. They could just be themselves, be silly with their feet, do a few twirls, and enjoy the music. In the midst of this musical chaos, I looked over at the two teachers – they were amazed; their mouths were slightly open! They seemed to be saying, "How did you do that?"

About a week later, while I was sitting with the kids, having lunch in the center cafeteria, one of the teachers came over to my table mumbling something very negative and ugly to me (she did that a lot). Her words felt like a wire brush deep inside my soul, scraping up and down. Whenever one of the teachers spoke in such a negative tone to me, I tried to respond in precisely the opposite manner: with a positive, nurturing answer. After my response to her, she yelled at me at the top of her lungs in front of everybody declaring, "Karen, I am sick and tired of hearing good things from you!"

What could I possibly say to that?

This center was awash in destructive talk; the poisoned attitudes of the teachers polluted the words and attitudes of their impressionable students.

THE LIGHT SIDE

Oh how I looked forward to working my two days a week on the near side of the river! Not only did I get to skip the treacherous ferry ride across the Mississippi River (about a year later a ferry capsized and killed most of the riders), but I also experienced a totally different atmosphere. The teacher at this center was young, fresh out of college, with an outgoing personality.

Lucy loved life; it was obvious to all of us who worked with her that she also loved her job. This center, like the one across the river, had about fifteen students. But the similarities between the two centers stopped there.

Lucy's kids would step off the bus in the morning, walk in happy, talking to each other and the teacher; peppy music played in the background. They greeted the staff with hugs, and would always ask, "How are you today, Miss Karen?"

One morning when the music was on, I grabbed Joseph by the hand because I knew he loved to dance fast. The other kids stood around us, clapping their hands, cheering us on, wanting more. Even the teachers participated, clapping their hands, yelling out, "Go, Joseph, go."

The difference between the two centers was the difference between dark and light. I loved teaching the students at the light center simple things, like how to count change. "This is a dime, and here is a quarter. If you add the two together, how much money do you have?"

"A lot," one student answered.

We'd test each student, and when one student tried hard and cooperated, everybody would applaud and say, "Good job. Good job." If somebody spilled something, Lucy would laugh, reassure the embarrassed spiller that "It's okay," then have several other students join in to help clean up the mess.

Fear did not dwell in these kids.

The students enjoyed participating in everything going on, so when the Special Olympics came to town, they became deeply involved as runners, jumpers or helpers, and it didn't matter if they won or lost.

Lucy started a hothouse to grow tomato plants as one of her many projects; everyone was given a job in the hothouse so they could feel important. Some planted seeds, others watered, and some sold the tomatoes when they were ripe.

Many times Lucy would have one of the students stand up in front of the entire group and share something funny that had happened. It was a heartwarming experience for the teachers and the students alike because there was such an open freedom in their sharing, with no fear of criticism or condemnation.

All of these positive student experiences were diligently documented in their case files as a permanent record of the positive ways they responded to life.

One day after a wonderful lunch (we all ate at the same cafeteria as the Catholic school that housed us), we sat around feeling stuffed and lazy, relaxing and talking in our free time. What a sight we made! Some students were quite old, in their sixties. One young man, in his twenties, was on crutches; every age from eighteen on up was in that center. In the midst of the casual relaxation, I stood up, stretched my arms, and announced, "I'm going on a walk. Does anybody want to come with me?"

To my dilemma and complete surprise, everybody stood up. Lucy looked over at me and yelled across the room, "Go ahead, Miss Karen. Have a good time. See you later."

What a fun place to work!

What incredible teachers to work with.

An absolute joy permeated that center.

I called that center "the light side", and the other, "the dark side" (this was even before Star Wars). Each center reflected darkness or light from the moment I entered.

24

The attitudes, words and thoughts conveyed on the dark center produced unhappiness, loneliness, and an absence of joy.

Ungodly self-talk (criticism and negativism) dominated the darkness.

On the light side, the words, thoughts and actions were a breath of encouragement, laughter and joy for all.

These two centers dramatically illustrated to me, firsthand, the importance in day-to-day living of the godly self-talk principles I will share in this book.

God's principles ALWAYS work – with the rich, the poor, the smart or the mentally challenged. God's grace, and His principles, are for us all...and they work in ALL situations and circumstances.

CHAPTER TWO

Kick the Baby Off the Cliff

Mike and I and our three boys only lived in Louisiana for eighteen months. We had uprooted our lives in Santa Maria, California and moved to Louisiana with the good intentions of attempting to minister to the people in Gramercy, a small town midway between New Orleans and Baton Rouge.

Eighteen months later, our ministry was in shambles, Mike's sales were failing badly, and we were not able to make our monthly mortgage payments. Even money for daily groceries and gas for the car became a struggle. Without money or hope, we knew we had to leave Louisiana, abandoning the home we had purchased (ultimately, it was repossessed by the bank), and forfeiting Mike's construction sales business, T. Lord's Tool Company.

So depressing were the ugly events of those eighteen months that Mike had grown suicidal. We left Gramercy in a rush, literally fleeing from bill collectors (a very long story for another book). We also left behind Mike's work van and all the equipment and supplies he had purchased and used for his tool supply business. They were ultimately sold by the bank for mere pennies. We drove the road back to California discouraged, broke and broken.

In Louisiana, we had lived in a large, 4,000 square foot home; when we arrived back in California, Mike and I and our three boys moved in with my Mom and Dad in their home in Santee for five months; we occupied two very small bedrooms.

We felt humbled, disgraced and abandoned by God.

After living on welfare for the next three months (Mike and I were both too emotionally battered to even think about working), Mike (still on anti-depressants) finally landed his first writing job with Morris Cerullo World Evangelism in San Diego, California. The year was 1981. A couple of months later we were able to move out of my parents' home and into a small rental house.

As we tried to adjust to our new lives, desperately attempting to sort out the recent devastation of the Louisiana experience, I began to realize how much deep anger I had toward God.

"Lord, how could You lead us to Louisiana only for us to lose everything? What kind of God would do that to His children?"

"Lord, how could You reduce my husband to the place where he sat on a bed in Louisiana with a shotgun pointed at his head, determined to die?"

"Lord, how could You put my three, innocent kids through such a devastating 'adventure'?"

Tormented by these and other destructive thoughts, I finally decided I couldn't stand the way I was feeling anymore. Somehow, I instinctively seemed to know what I had to do.

Every morning I knelt down on my knees and spoke to God saying, "Lord, I have all this anger toward You inside of me, and I can't seem to make it go away. But through You, I know all things are possible. So, please Lord, help take this anger away. I just don't want to be angry with You anymore."

One morning, after six months of praying that prayer every day – with no relief, I was walking through the living room.

What was that? What's that new feeling? I whispered to myself. *Oh my God, there's no anger!*

This unfamiliar feeling so jolted me that I stopped abruptly in the middle of the living room, feet planted, clutching a toy I had just picked up. For the first time

29

in six months there was no anger in me when I thought about God! I spent the rest of the day appreciating the relief, thanking and praising God for His deliverance from this anger.

IT JUST *LOOKS* INNOCENT

Despite my prayer breakthrough, there was so much more going on in my mind that kept me from being victorious. At the time I believed my life and purpose were limited to *just* serving my husband and children. I loved being a mom and a wife, but there was no joy in my heart because I diminished that role rather than reveling in it; it became a struggle to get through the day.

One morning, in the midst of my continuing depression, I heard God speak to me about the things I was doing, and was responsible for, that were contributing to my depression. He showed me a mental picture of a little baby, about nine months old, sitting on a very high cliff that looked like the Grand Canyon. The baby's legs were dangling over the side of that huge canyon.

From a distance, I could only see the back of the baby. As I walked closer, I noticed that the baby had small horns protruding from its head, and a long tail. As I walked closer to that quickly changing baby, I could hear God say to me..."Kick the baby off the cliff."

Being the obedient servant I am, I immediately questioned God, asking, "But, why Lord?"

"It looks innocent, but it's not," He patiently replied.

Somehow, I intuitively understood the meaning of His simple, yet life-changing message, and kicked that baby in the butt, right off the cliff!

Later, while trying to decipher the full meaning of that visual experience, God showed me that my thoughts, like the little baby, often seemed innocent enough. But, if they are ungodly (destructive) thoughts (with horns and a tail), they will produce only devastation and death. That little picture helped me to begin to understand how important it was to *take every thought captive* (2 Corinthians 10:5), kicking out the ungodly self-talk in my life.

At the start of this book I wrote out the text of Mark 7:14-23 from The Living Bible. I am going to repeat it here, and once again I'm going to ask you to read it out loud. Let this life-changing biblical concept start to seep deep into your spirit!

> *Then Jesus called to the crowd to come and hear. "All of you listen," he said, "and try to understand. Your souls aren't harmed by what you eat, but by what you think and say!"*

> *Then he went into a house to get away from the*

31

crowds, and his disciples asked him what he meant by the statement he had just made.

"Don't you understand either?" he asked. "Can't you see that what you eat won't harm your soul? For food doesn't come in contact with your heart, but only passes through the digestive system." (By saying this he showed that every kind of food is kosher.)

And then he added, "<u>It is the thought-life that pollutes</u>. For from within, out of men's hearts, come evil thoughts of lust, theft, murder, adultery, wanting what belongs to others, wickedness, deceit, lewdness, envy, slander, pride, and all other folly. All these vile things come from within; <u>they are what pollute you and make you unfit for God</u>."

What you think and say impacts your soul! Your thought life can pollute or prosper, depending upon how well you monitor your thought life and learn how to "kick the baby off the cliff" in your own life.

PRODUCTIVE, YET STILL MISERABLE?

I shared the story of how God told me to "kick the baby off the cliff" with my husband, but he didn't seem very impressed. He mumbled something like, "That's nice, honey," then continued to read his newspaper.

The next day we went to church. Throughout the entire service my legs were crossed, with one leg slightly jerking up and down like I was nervous or agitated. My husband put his hand on my knee and whispered, "Honey are you nervous? You keep moving your leg up and down."

"No, I'm not nervous," I whispered back with a slight smile, "I'm just kicking the baby off the cliff."

To my amazement, during that church service there was a steady stream of negative, self-degrading thoughts that kept passing through my mind; I kicked constantly!

Later, as I learned how to *Kick the Baby Off the Cliff*, the Holy Spirit showed me this alarming, amazing revelation:

> A person can be saved, delivered from bondages, filled with the Holy Spirit, love and serve God, have a ministry...AND STILL BE MISERABLE!

Even pastors, elders and Bible teachers deal with this issue. We don't ever arrive. We need to constantly monitor this area of godly and ungodly self-talk.

INNOCENT CONDEMNATION

Ungodly self-talk starts with a seemingly innocent, self-condemning statement that relates to the past, present or future.

"I never was any good, I'm not any good now, and I'll never be able to change."

Or, your thoughts may be more subtle, such as constantly seeing yourself from a negative point of view.

"If I talk, they will find out how stupid and misinformed I am."

"If I wear something baggy today, perhaps people won't notice that I am fat."

The solution for these ungodly thoughts is to shift your mind to godly thinking. Once you recognize the lie, you have the God-given power to stop pouring poison on your mind; you possess His ability to replace the ungodly thought with one more in line with His Holy Word, and more consistent with His loving heart toward you.

CHAPTER THREE

The Painful Visit

Whenever our friends from the Philippines, Eddie and Dory Villanueva, came to visit us, I was always initially excited about their coming...until about the second day after they arrived. I viewed them as giants in the ministry, godly people...and they were.

Brother Eddie (as he is still affectionately called by his congregation) founded J.I.L. Fellowship (Jesus is Lord Fellowship), which grew from a few hundred to a church with several thousand pastors (yes, thousand) and hundreds of thousands of members in the Philippines, and around the world (one of the largest churches in the world).

When Eddie and Dory visited our home with their team members, they were always interested in what my husband had to say. They had a stirring story they wanted to tell, and they wanted Mike, as a Christian author, to write it!

Brother Eddie was once a radical, Communist activist who, in his college days, led over one million youth in the Communist Party. After his conversion to Christianity, he asked the Lord to "Allow me to lead one million people to You."

Thankfully, these stays with us were seldom more than a few days because, when Brother Eddie came to the U.S., he had family and church members in other parts of California to visit. Eddie was not only the leader of J.I.L. Fellowship in the Philippines, but he also oversaw sister churches in San Diego, Los Angeles, Canada, England and Hong Kong. His one sister led the church in Los Angeles, and another sister pastored a church in Carson, California.

It seemed everyone in the family pastored a church!

When the Villanueva family came to stay at our home, those who came with them were also deeply involved in ministry. It would be a vast understatement to say that in the midst of their ministry magnitude, I felt insignificant.

FEELING DIRTY

The first day of their visit was usually full of greetings, gifts, love and compliments; they shared story after story of funny, exciting or dramatic incidents happening in the Philippines. In one such sharing we learned how Brother Eddie's life, and the lives of his family members, were endangered when a bomb exploded on the front porch of their family home, reportedly planted by Communist rebels in the Philippines.

As stories unfolded, I dove into the homemaking process where I felt most secure...cooking dinners, breakfasts, etc., for the large groups. Then, I'd fluff up the pillows, change the sheets, and put the group up for the night.

Homemaking was my expertise!

I knew how to welcome guests and cook great meals (remember, I *am* Italian). However, by the next day, as the conversations continued, I began to feel distant, not wanting to be in the same room as the group. I actually believed I was somehow spiritually "dirty" around such godly people.

Old, destructive thoughts started pouring out their deadly poison.

"They're not interested in talking to me."

"I'm only good for cooking the meals."

"They are not even bothering to look my way anymore."

"I can see I am no longer needed, or even wanted in this room."

"Everyone else except me has a ministry in common, including my husband Mike, the Christian writer."

These times of hosting inevitably led to the beginnings of my own self-talk sabotage.

PARALYZED BY LIES

By the afternoon of the second day I could barely speak to the group. In fact, I was now resentful that they were even in my home! The ungodly messages in my head all morning and all afternoon brought me down to a sudden, deep depression.

"I am in the way."

"I have nothing to offer".

"I'm not as good as these people – they know it and I know it."

Their goodness made me feel unworthy to even be in the same room. These feelings grew stronger and stronger until I finally found myself hating who I was.

Jealousy rose up.

Every time they would have a glowing report about Michael, a little more hatred was born in my heart for my precious husband. They complimented him soooo much that it made me feel smaller, swallowed up.

Nauseated. The bigger Mike was, the smaller I felt. My spirit became a sore, an open wound, and they were vigorously rubbing stinging salt granules into it.

The more they exalted Mike, the more it devastated me.

Within 24 hours I became a different person, ready to cry at any moment. I was depressed, wanting to avoid people, to hide and not be that perfect hostess, that person who welcomes guests and makes them feel comfortable. I wanted to flee to a distant hideaway and not be with them anymore. Somehow, I knew I'd be better off when they left, but not until then.

A few weeks after one such visit, I discussed my emotions with an ex-pastor who was now a psychologist and counselor. I explained to him how I felt about these visits every year, always believing that the next visit would be somehow different.

"Karen, you don't know how much you are loved by God," he told me. "That's why you feel the way you do."

One morning I gave some serious thought to what the counselor said, asking God, "Lord, is that true? I know about You, I read about You, and I know in my head that You love me. But Lord, today I want to ask You to help me transfer that knowledge in my head to my heart. Please show me how much You love me. If this is my problem, please help me."

39

For the next week, God started to pour out His love, showing me in situation after situation how much He loved me! It was like I had a new pair of eyes to see. God seemed to go out of His way to show me that the things I said and did every single day were an intimate part of my experience of Him. There was a growing knowing in my spirit that "God cares deeply about me." The Holy Spirit cleared away cobwebs inside my soul; my new spiritual ears began to hear God say, "Karen Judith Wourms, you are a very special lady in My eyes, and you don't have to do anything special or big in ministry to earn My favor. I like you just the way you are."

By the end of that week I was overwhelmed by the warmth and mind-blowing awareness of God in my life! For the first time I began to understand how precious I was to Him. My self-importance in life was rooted in His love for me, not in what I accomplished in ministry.

A year went by after this prayer to the Father when Mike announced to me, "Our Filipino friends are coming next month. Would you like me to have them stay somewhere else?" he asked, giving me the opportunity to avoid the deep depression that was always activated by their stay.

"Absolutely not!" I replied. "I am looking forward to their visit."

"You are kidding? What about how hard it is for you?" Mike asked with confusion and doubt.

"Nope, I'm different," I confidently answered.

And, the Villanueva's next visit was indeed different. Because my value was rooted in God's love for me, I now realized how much I had to offer. I talked so much I was worried that I might be interfering with their conversations! As I viewed myself as a person loved by God, I confidently thought to myself... *"You've got to hear this, you will want to hear this, I've got something of value to say."*

Whenever any sliver of that old, depressing, ungodly self-talk started to slip in, I would declare, "Nope, I'm not going there. God thinks I am valuable, so I must be. They're lucky to know me."

When you start to diminish yourself through ungodly self-talk, remember, God wants you to know how much He loves you; He considers you to be the apple of His eye, and protects you under the shadow of His wings.

Keep me as the apple of the eye, hide me under the shadow of thy wings.

(Psalm 17:8)

CHAPTER FOUR

Pouring Poison on Your Plants

Much happened in the subsequent eight years following our degrading return from Louisiana. My two oldest boys were newly married to lovely ladies; the weddings took place within two months of each other. As a result of both sons leaving home so close to each other, I became the classic case of a mother experiencing "the empty-nest syndrome"...an overwhelming feeling of emptiness permeated my life.

Even though I still had one teenager, Mitch, living with us and going to high school, I absolutely believed that my life as a mother (the only life I had ever known) was over. Each day I lived as though the "mom" part of my life had died. Mitch was now going to Mike, my husband, for advice more frequently than he came to me. I understood, in my head, that Mitch's need to separate from his Mom and become close to his

Dad was a normal process, but that did not stop my heart from aching. The almost empty house just didn't seem like "home" anymore.

A Purposeless Life

Getting up in the morning became an empty, futile exercise; I had seemingly lost my purpose – being a mom – something I had wanted more than anything else in my life since the time I was a very young girl.

Mike was growing stronger in his walk with the Lord; his writing and consulting business was doing well. He no longer needed me to hold him up. For the first thirteen years of our marriage I had functioned as the strong one while Mike secured, and then lost, twenty-one different jobs (yes, that too is another book).

Up to this moment, my entire life's energy had been poured into serving my husband and children. Being a mother defined who I was: mom and wife. These two roles made me happy and gave me a sense of purpose. Now, both of these functions had dramatically shifted...no, disappeared.

Every morning was the same...I'd get up, go sit in my special chair by the window in the living room and pick up a spiritual book to read, searching for some semblance of encouragement or meaning. Then, I'd pick up my Bible and read God's Word, all the while feeling low, blue. My subsequent prayer time was spent begging and pleading with God to take away this sad and fatalistic feeling I had about life.

Each day I sank a little deeper into depression.

Yet, every day I faithfully followed the same futile ritual of reading and prayer! But frankly, these rituals were not doing much good. I must confess, I was even disappointed at God for the cruel trick He had played on me, creating me for the sake of Mike and my kids, and when they no longer needed me, He had abandoned me as easily as a gardener dispenses with a useless, broken rake when it has outlived its purpose.

My depressing thoughts translated into my pathetic, desperate prayers.

"Lord, why don't You just take me? I've done my job. I've raised my family. My boys don't need me anymore. Mike is productive in his work and doesn't need my support. In fact, nobody in this family needs me anymore. I'm done. I'm not good for anything else, so Lord, please take me. Amen."

GARDEN LESSONS

After my spiritual readings and morning prayer rituals, I would usually go outside into the backyard to hand-water the flowers in my garden. I really enjoyed the time I spent in my garden! Since it was still early morning, I'd usually go out dressed in my green, silky robe, with a cup of coffee in one hand and a watering hose in the other, doing the one remaining purposeful task each day that gave me pleasure: watering my garden.

As the water poured out on the plants, my mind would wallow in negative thoughts and feelings.

"Here I am, starting another long day of meaningless chores, with no sense of purpose."

"Here I am, and the only thing I'm good for anymore is holding this stupid water hose to pour water on these plants. Big deal. An automatic sprinkler could replace my life."

On one particular morning, when I came in from watering my garden, and wallowing in my thoughts, Mike was standing in the kitchen looking like he had something to say. As I poured another cup of coffee, he timidly spoke as though he were afraid of how I would react to what he was going to share.

"Karen, God's told me something that He wants me to tell you."

All I could think was...

"Oh, no, it can't be good. God's going to ball me out. What am I headed for now?"

My other thought reflected resentment.

"If God has something to tell me, why doesn't He

come straight to me? Aren't I even important enough to tell it to directly?"

Mike could see the apprehension on my face, so he spoke to me in a loving, kind tone, understanding that what he was about to share was not flattering, and might make things actually more difficult for me.

POISON'S NOT FOR GROWTH

"Honey, when you were watering your flowers, the Lord told me, 'The water she is pouring on her flowers won't help them grow because it is poison.'"

I looked at Mike and snapped, "What's that supposed to mean?"

Then Mike shared a bit more.

"Well, I believe it means that those negative things you are telling yourself all day long are like pouring poison on the garden of your mind. You can saturate your plants all you want with poisoned water, but they won't grow, and eventually, they will die.

"Karen, I think God is saying that you can read as much of the Word as you want, you can pray faithfully each day, pleading with God to change you, but all of your desperate prayers won't work until you stop pouring poison on your mind with your ungodly self-talk."

47

"Thanks a lot," I sarcastically replied. "Do you think that's really going to help me? Do you think that has anything to do with why I feel depressed? Do you think such nonsense is really my problem?"

I went over to my window and plopped down in my rocking chair, very angry inside about what God was supposedly saying to me.

It couldn't be that simple!

I knew what I was feeling each day was real!

I had every reason to believe and feel that things were as bad as they were.

I <u>knew</u> the <u>truth</u>, and God was sadly mistaken!

I sat there for awhile, then I suddenly wondered:

"What if this is true? I don't believe it is, but... just what if it is true?"

"O.K. God, I'm gonna make a deal with You. I'll give You one week. I will correct every bit of ungodly, self-talk poison that comes into my mind by replacing it with a godly statement. But, I am asking You to help me recognize when I do it."

"Now, God, You understand I don't believe this stuff is going to work, but I'm still making the deal. Amen."

REPLACING THE POISON

After my "deal" with God, I got up from my rocking chair and went into the kitchen, knowing I had several hours of work to do there. As I began my first chore, I immediately noticed that ungodly thoughts started their pathetic parade into my mind. As I was sweeping the floor, my thought was,

"My left-over life is reduced to sweeping the floor. Big deal."

I stopped my thought and corrected the poison.

"No, I am more than a floor sweeper. My life does have some meaning."

Admittedly, that short statement felt foreign, even like a lie, but in obedience to God, I was going to try this new way of thinking.

As I was doing the dishes, I thought,

"Who wants to know you? You're ugly!"

Once again I stopped pouring the poison.

"No! I can look pretty good when I take the time to fix myself up. I clean up pretty good."

The battles between what I now call "ungodly self-talk" and "godly self-talk" went on and on for the next two hours – the kitchen floor was not the only place that needed a deep cleaning that day.

49

After two hours of this life-changing exercise, I realized that I had spewed out at least a hundred negative (ungodly) thoughts! Up to that afternoon, I had absolutely no idea that my mind was so busy manufacturing putrid poison, negative thoughts about my future, about how I distorted yesterday, and how I so willingly diminished today.

I was swimming in a putrid pool of emotional vomit.

In obedience to God, I faithfully corrected every single negative self-talk by replacing it with godly, positive self-talk. Frankly, it wasn't easy to think godly thoughts because I didn't believe anything good about myself; I was not comfortable thinking that way.

The negative felt so right, so true...so much like the real me. I felt I was fighting from within the deepest part of me – the core that represented who I was. For two hours I spoke words that went against my core beliefs; I spoke godly words that felt like lies about who I was.

The false "truth" I had held onto was so much more comfortable to me, even though it was poisonous and destructive.

I soon began to recognize how firmly grounded I had become in ungodly talk.

I soon began to realize that my version of "truth" was nothing more than subtle, poisoned water I had been pouring by the gallon on my mind.

Throughout the rest of the day, the nagging, self-degrading self-talk continued.

And so did the correcting.

Every time I spoke a negative, I rebuked it, and then replaced it with the best version of godly self-talk I could muster at the moment. It was as though there was a person on the outside of me looking at me, telling me "Here are a few good things about you," but they had no connection to my reality as I saw it.

I <u>didn't feel</u> the godly self-talk was me, but I had made a promise to God to remove the poison and replace it with godly talk. My core person inside still felt comfortable grumbling allllll daaaay looooong – because that old core was my most comfortable self-pity position – the one I knew, the one I believed and clutched onto as the real truth.

EMERGING FROM THE DARK

That first day was the hardest.

The second day produced dramatically less negative self-talk in my head; my mood actually started to feel a little bit better. The depression wasn't overwhelming anymore.

51

By the third day, there were only a few times when the ungodly self-talk popped up. I noticed that I was starting to feel more alive, even glad, to be on this earth. Each successive day presented less and less degradation and more and more times of peace.

By the seventh day, the negative self-talk had disappeared! In its place there was an unfamiliar, new feeling...almost euphoria. I began to think,

"There's a whole new world out there. What do I want to accomplish in it?"

I knew there were many things I had never done or tried to do, or even dared to dream that I could do, that I suddenly wanted to do now.

Somehow, for the first time in my life, I figured it was time to try some of them!

CHAPTER FIVE

Stretching New Wings

Ambitions that had died or that had been buried long ago, suddenly seemed possible! A new attitude possessed me. "I can do anything I want to do if I stick it out" was my new, triumphant declaration that soaked deep into my spirit and soul.

Before my transformation process, when Mike would ask, "Honey, what are your dreams?" I'd answer curtly, "I don't dream. If I did, I'd only be disappointed."

Now dreams suddenly seemed real...and obtainable.

FROM MOTHER TO COUNSELOR

One dream I had secretly lodged in my heart was

to do something I considered worthwhile – beyond being a mother, cooking and doing housework. Now I do understand and value motherhood – being a mother is all I ever wanted to be. I do understand the importance of providing a warm, secure home for the family. Cooking and housework are meaningful, and I still do both each and every day. But after twenty-six years in the same job description, I was ready for a new challenge. My desire now was not to just continue doing the things I had proven proficient in doing, but to seek out new, meaningful challenges.

One day my husband presented me with three typed pages of non-profit organizations in San Diego, California; it listed their phone numbers and addresses.

"Honey, this is the list of Christian organizations you asked for. Perhaps you might be interested in helping as a volunteer at one of them," he said, knowing I wanted to try some new things. I called every single organization on those three pages, but only one returned my call.

"Yes, we have an opening here at the San Diego Pregnancy Services for a counselor," the lady on the other end of the phone told me. "If you are interested in that position, we will be starting a new training class in a few days."

Could I?

Dare I?

Of course I could...because I was in the process of becoming the new Karen (Ephesians 4:24).

I took the training class (shaking and full of uncertainty), and soon was placed in a counseling position that proved to be yet another major step toward fulfilling my long-delayed dreams which were now starting to come true.

For the next three-and-a-half years I had the privilege of working with young, distraught, pregnant women, helping guide their lives and lovingly steering them away from the long-term ravages that would result if they selected the "abortion alternatives" of Planned Parenthood and other pro-abortion organizations.

PERFORM IN A PLAY?

At the time of this unexpected transformation process, I was attending a local church in La Mesa, California that placed a heavy emphasis on bringing to the community professionally presented Gospel plays. One Sunday morning they announced, "We are going to hold auditions for our annual Easter play."

Something jumped in my spirit. I had always wanted to be in the limelight, to ham it up, to perform in a play! Now, at forty-six-years-old (my age then), I was suddenly anxious to jump on the stage and be a star for a night (Yeah, I know, my motives weren't the purest at that point.).

As a result of my audition, I was awarded a very small part. But something was alive in me that could not be contained or squelched. I was on fire! My eyes beamed confidence; my spirit soared. My small part grew as I added a few additional lines. During each performance, I just couldn't seem to help myself. Somehow I'd always end up standing in front on stage, having a wonderful time exploring and expanding my part.

When my church selected the cast for their next production, to my joy and surprise, they selected me as one of the main characters! I began to realize that this forty-six-year-old woman's dreams could come true as I dared to dream.

THE TICKERTAPE PARADE

Remember the experience I shared about my thought life in my kitchen, when God first revealed to me how my mind was polluted with ungodly thoughts? Well, about a year after that first two-hour kitchen experience, when I was driving home and turning off the freeway, I felt a slight lowness sneak into my spirit – not a depression, but a feeling of mild "blues" for no apparent reason. As I was turning off onto my street, I heard in my head ugly thoughts that went in one side and came out the other – as though my head were suddenly a human tickertape, displaying every vicious thing I ever said about myself...ungodly, destructive messages.

I sat and cringed, shaking for a few seconds as though I had a sudden chill. I said to myself,

"I can't believe that I once believed every one of those horrible lies I said so emphatically about myself."

God gave me that experience to demonstrate that I was different now; He allowed me to see how my life had become full of good things instead of so many self-fed, bad thoughts. That tickertape experience made me ask the question, "Lord, how did I ever get so bad?"

Only later did I begin to really understand how God was teaching me through His Holy Spirit what His Word already revealed in 2 Corinthians 10:5:

Therefore, I stand against Satan's deception by taking every thought captive in obedience to Christ.

"LORD, WHY ME?"

The next seed for a dream was first planted in me when I came back from a women's retreat with an excitement that "God was going to do something"...I just didn't know what. I kept asking, "Lord, what is this feeling of expectation that something is going to happen? It feels good, but what do I do with it?"

On one particular night shortly after the retreat, I was preparing to go to a women's meeting at the church where I had been asked to give a short testimony on "What the retreat meant to me." Earlier that afternoon I was down on my knees praying, "Lord, what in the world do You want me to share? How can I share anything about this expectation You have given me when I don't even know where it is going myself?"

Clearly, I didn't know what to say, or even if what I would say could have an ounce of value to anyone. If I couldn't make any sense out of my excitement, then how could anybody else?

But, I promised the lady I'd share.

Imagine, she never even asked me if I had a testimony! Yet, for some strange reason, when she asked, I replied excitedly, "Yes, I'll do it," wondering all the while what my excitement was about.

As I dressed that night, I again prayed, "Well, Lord, I haven't a clue what I'm going to say. Just give me the words."

That night many ladies gave testimonies on how the retreat impacted their lives. We were all supposed to give two or three minute little testimonies, but they were all drawing out a bit longer. When it was my turn, I still had no sense of what I was going to say, but I went up front in obedience.

"There's an expectation inside of me," I told the ladies, "that was birthed at the retreat, and I just can't seem to get rid of it. I am expecting it will lead me into something, but I have no idea what."

I thought that was it.

My testimony was over, but my mouth kept moving.

"And, I am so grateful to God because He has healed me from the ravages of my childhood abuse. I was molested as a child by a friend of the family. That experience devastated every part of my life. But through several years of being led by the healing power of the Holy Spirit, God has touched my life so profoundly that I am now healed. I am so grateful to God for my healing."

I had no idea why I said what I said. It felt like a continuation of my mouth going off without any control. I later learned that God would release His divine purpose, even through my shallow understanding.

At that point, the leader motioned with her hand for me to stop. I had definitely gone over my time, speaking for about five minutes! She politely said, "Thank you, Karen. Next."

After the meeting, I was surrounded by a group of excited ladies, some pulling on me to get my attention, others asking, "How did you get healed?"

I honestly didn't know what to say to them. They asked me things like, "Can you help me?" and "What did the Holy Spirit do?" As I stood in the midst of this excitement and chaos, I thought to myself,

> *"Lord, why me? Why are they asking me these questions? How do I answer them? Lord, it would be a great blessing to help others climb out of their destructive thoughts and self-degrading images, but how?"*

The night was overwhelming. Fourteen ladies spoke with me that night, seeking information on how they too could be healed. I went home thinking,

> *"Lord, what do I do with all of this?"*

CHAPTER SIX

"God's Trying to Tell You Something."

The next day I shared with my husband what happened at the women's meeting. The excitement from the fourteen women was such an unexpected result of the few minutes I shared. After hearing my report, Mike's first reply to me was, "Karen, God's trying to tell you something."

That same morning I received a phone call from one of the ladies at the women's meeting, asking for help. All the questions she asked I understood, and knew how to guide her. But, it was a surprise – even a shock – to me that I knew the answers.

I honestly didn't know I had any answers!

The phone calls kept coming that week, and God kept showing me that I knew how to answer their questions. I had no idea God had taught me so much.

The second week continued with more phone calls. Again, as I would hang up the phone, my husband would say, 'Karen, I'm telling you honey, God's trying to tell you something."

"It is not a divine coincidence that these people are calling," I replied. "These people heard me share for a few minutes on something important to them, so they are calling. It is only natural they would call out of curiosity, wanting to know what they can do for themselves."

Yet, Mike continued to remind me after every phone call, "Karen, I think you should take this seriously. I think God is really trying to tell you something. You'd better take another look at it."

THE RELUCTANT LOOK

With a heavy heart, and not really wanting to go in that direction, not really wanting God to say that this is something He wanted from me, I prayed despite my doubts:

"God, are You trying to tell me something? And if so, could You make it a little plainer for me? This stuff is serious! These women are suffering from serious issues, and I don't want to hurt any of them. I could actually make things worse. So, if there's something You want me to do, please make it very clear to me, because I don't always get it. Amen."

That day, after my prayer, the lady in charge of the women's counsel called me and asked if I would run a small group in the church for women who were hurting from childhood abuse.

"Oh my God, this is getting serious," I thought to myself. *"This isn't even fun anymore."* Yes, the calls gave me a sense of importance, but now I was experiencing fear.

"Where are You leading me, Lord?" I asked. "This doesn't seem like something I want to get into. It is much too serious for a woman like me. I don't have a college degree, or credentials in this subject. I'm not qualified."

The lady gave me a week to think about her offer. I didn't know if this group was from God, but I did know that fear was running through my body.

The calls kept coming in; they showed me that this was certainly an unmet need in our church. I was surprised how many women were still hurting deeply from childhood abuse, and did not know how to climb out of their pain.

Again, Michael would say, "Well, Karen, do you

now have enough proof that God is directing you to lead a group? Do you have enough verification from God?"

"Michael, it is natural women would call after I told them that I had been healed," I stubbornly replied. "I am not that sure it is from God."

Frankly, it terrified me to think that it might be. It wasn't even a pleasant thought anymore.

"Lord, I know all the phone calls could be proof, but they could also be the natural response after hearing about my story. So, please, Father, I need You to do a biggie, something so that I cannot deny that this is where you want me to go. So God, please give me a biggie. Amen."

What a woman of faith I was! Shaking in my boots, I was hoping that God did not want me to do anything at all in this area. Yet, there was a pull inside of me; I wanted to be used by God beyond my ministry as a homemaker and a wife.

I wanted a calling from God – but I just didn't want this one. After all, I had no training, and only a high school degree. I raised my three boys, but never saw myself qualified for much of anything else but motherhood.

That night, God answered my prayer for "a biggie".

THE BIGGIE

I was in the Easter play that night at church (yes, the result of my first audition), and in between scenes, we had a very large classroom where we all gathered when we were not on stage. I brought a book with me to read because I had a small, yet ever-increasing part in the play, which left me plenty of reading time. There were about forty minutes before my next scene, so I took out my book and started to read. At the time, there were about forty people in the room with me, talking, readjusting their costumes and putting on make-up.

I sat at the far end of a couch in a corner of the room, resting my arm on its arm, and started to read. I looked up from my book when I sensed something strange. What I saw amazed me. Virtually everyone in that room was standing in front of me, looking at the book.

One voice came from the group, asking,

"What are you reading?"

"*Pain and Pretending* by Rich Buehler," I replied.

"What's it about?" another asked.

"About people who have been abused as children."

'Why are you reading it?" another voice asked.

"I'm thinking about doing a healing workshop for women with childhood abuse," I answered.

65

One lady literally grabbed the book out of my hand and went to the other corner of the room and started to read it.

A sweet, tall, dark and very handsome young man, dressed as Judas, knelt down beside me. He took my one hand and gently put it into his two hands. With tears in his eyes, he looked at me and pleaded, "Please, please, I beg you, do this class. I have a dear friend who has tried to commit suicide several times, and I know that her childhood abuse is the reason for her depression. Please, please do the class."

I was more than overwhelmed that evening; I stood in awe of how God orchestrated all of this to speak to me personally. This was no coincidence; it was a divine appointment.

"BUT LORD, I'M NOT QUALIFIED."

You'd think by now I was absolutely convinced, right? What a powerful woman of God I am.

Not so.

By the time I woke up the next day, my thoughts were,

"I don't want to do this. I'm not qualified. I can't lead people who are hurting so desperately when I don't have a clue what to do."

66

God was so powerful the night before, and I was so weak and shaking. It was not that I didn't want to do it...I was scared to do it. But because God looks at the heart, I know He forgave me for my weakness.

Later that day I received that final phone call from the lady in charge of small groups.

"Karen, have you made up your mind about doing that healing workshop for women?"

"I don't know. I really don't know."

At this point, because God knew me so intimately well, He tricked me into saying yes.

"Well, if you don't do it, I will, and I think we should include any woman who has been abused, such as women abused by their husbands, in that class too."

That statement struck me like a lightning bolt.

This lady had a good heart, but she didn't understand that abuse in childhood comes from a whole different perspective. The ungodly decisions a child makes about herself after being abused are a vastly different situation than the wife who is abused by her husband.

Suddenly, I wanted to rescue every woman who would be in that class from a lack of understanding. And so, in order to protect these women from someone who really did not understand the nuances of childhood abuse, I blurted out, "Yes, I'll do it."

When I put down the phone I thought,

"God, You tricked me. Now what do I do?"

CHAPTER SEVEN

"Why Don't You Want the Ministry I Have Given You?"

After all the clear signs God had given me that He indeed wanted me to go ahead with the class, and after all the phone calls of confirmation I had received, when the Healing Workshop for Women with Childhood Abuse was finally announced, two ladies signed up.

A bit discouraged, I thought to myself,

"Well, I still have to be faithful. And Lord, if this wasn't You, I'm still going to act like it was You. I'm going to do the class anyway, even if I still don't know what to do."

The class was scheduled to run about eight weeks; three weeks into it, only one lady remained, but what a marvelous time we had together! We prayed and talked. She experienced deliverance, healing of emotions, forgiveness; the Holy Spirit ministered powerfully to her in our unexpected, very personal, one-on-one experience.

When I look back on that first class, I believe God was testing my faithfulness, essentially asking me, "Karen, whether there's one or twenty in your class, are you going to be faithful and obedient as a vessel I can use and trust?"

Still not convinced that anyone would come to the next class if I ran the announcement again, I took another step of faith, out of obedience, not really looking forward to the next class, almost hoping only a few would sign up.

Seventeen ladies responded; I immediately fell to my knees.

"Okay, God, what do I do with seventeen ladies?" I prayed. "You know this is a lot different than a one-on-one experience. What do You want me to do for these next eight weeks? Amen."

God instantly showed me His program, using the experiences I had gone through as the basis for the teaching. He outlined what I was to do on every night, and how to do it – except for the first night.

I so clearly remember sitting in my bathtub that morning, knowing seventeen women were coming to my home that evening, and I still didn't have any notion of what to do with them that first night. So, as a powerful, faith-filled woman of God, I prayed,

> "Well, Lord, I've got seventeen women coming tonight. I guess we're just going to sit around and look at each other because You haven't told me what to do yet. Amen."

Instantly, He showed me the program for that night. How foolish I felt; how faithless I had been, and how powerful that first night turned out to be.

THE THREE-YEAR PRAYER

After three years of teaching the class, I still felt much like a music director conducting a symphony without really understanding how the music comes out so sweet. Yes, women were being healed and delivered, but something still troubled me, so I prayed:

> "Lord, as You know, I have this nagging thought in me that I shouldn't be doing this workshop. I'm not smart enough to under-stand what is going on here. What about using Margo, my partner? She is much more spiri-

tual than I am. Lord, I'm not qualified to do this class. Amen."

Imagine...after three years of watching God work in two classes per year, after three years of powerful healings and deliverances of women from the bondages of their childhoods, I still believed I was the wrong leader, and even had come to a place where I dreaded doing the class, always afraid the women would suffer due to my lack of ability.

Didn't the Lord know how unqualified I was?

GOD'S REBUKE

Before my fourth year of starting the class, I went to a church meeting where our pastors were praying for the leadership of our church. When my pastor came to pray over me, I'll never forget the words Pastor Dave spoke through the Holy Spirit:

"Why don't you want the ministry I have given you? I have given you everything you need."

He almost yelled out that strong Word from God! Suddenly, I felt so ashamed. That Word served to verify that God wanted me to continue teaching; Pastor Dave had absolutely no idea of the internal struggle I was having concerning the workshop.

My self-talk had been wretched, degrading the wonderful ministry God had entrusted to me.

After this simple, yet powerful Word from the Lord, I felt ashamed, and owed God an apology for my weakness and doubt. I apologized to God, and for the rest of my years teaching the class, I thanked Him for His ministry, praying things like,

> "Thank You, Lord, for blessing me with this class. It is a good thing You are doing the classes with me. Through You, I can do all things. Thank You for Your awesome blessings and trust in me. Amen."

That healing workshop continued twice a year for fifteen years; I've personally had the privilege of putting over five hundred women through this God-given healing process (including a strong lesson on how to walk in godly self-talk!). God has graciously allowed me to train up other women in the Body of Christ who are now continuing to release healing into other women's lives.

HERE I WAS...

My life continued to rapidly and incredibly change; I wanted to pinch myself to make sure I wasn't dreaming. I just kept asking, "Is this really happening to me?" I honestly never thought I would ever be anything else but a mom and a wife.

Yet, here I was...

Without a college education, a very simple, down-to-earth mother of three, counseling young, pregnant women in this critical time of their lives, helping them make life and death decisions such as, "How can I possibly keep this baby?"

Here I was...

Running a women's group dealing with extremely serious issues from childhood abuse, issues that had been repressed, in some cases, for ten, twenty or even forty years! Yet, God used Margo, my friend and partner, and me to teach, pray and release healing into these desperate women. We had the pleasure of seeing them transformed from their fears and insecurities to start their new lives without bondages and self-hate, to experience a new and better beginning.

Here I was...

A simple housewife whom God had somehow allowed the joy of teaching Marriage God's Way classes with my husband to hundreds of couples in our church, in retreats, and even in a Pastor's Conference in Cuba!

Thanks to the teaching of His Holy Spirit, and His life-transforming godly self-talk, my life had been miraculously transformed!

CHAPTER EIGHT

The Destructive Power of Ungodly Self-Talk

Self-talk involves those things you say about yourself and about your circumstances...past, present and future. Self-talk entails the things you tell yourself all day long about your life...and that talk has the power to build up or to destroy (Proverb 18:21).

Most self-talk is marred by untruths formed early in our childhood which we forever try to label as our "truth," even when we become adults. Some examples of ungodly self-talk include:

"Why should I try? I'll never become anything worthwhile."

"Good things happen to others, but they never happen to me."

"I hate my life."

"God obviously doesn't care about me. Otherwise, my life wouldn't be so miserable."

"I'm destined to be a failure. Nothing I do ever turns out right."

"I'm not smart enough to succeed."

"I'm too fat to be loveable."

"I'm too ugly to be in any form of ministry."

"I'm too dumb to witness the Gospel to others."

"People don't like me. They'd much rather talk to others than to me."

"I'm not lovable – even to myself."

Sound familiar?

If you have ever thought or said any of these statements, or if you can add your own litany of destructive "truths" to this list, you need to know that God has given you the **gift of control** over your mind (2 Corinthians 10:5). He created and designed you, so He knows that what you think and what you say have an impact over your life (Deuteronomy 30:12-20).

FACTS AND CONCLUSIONS

Even though God has given you that gift of control, one of the most challenging things you can ever do is learn how to **exercise that gift** by changing your ungodly self-talk (those things that go against His Word and His principles) to productive, godly self-talk that aligns with the teachings of His Word.

When I discuss these concepts with a person I am counseling, the first statement I usually hear is, "But Karen, what I say about myself **is** true." They then proceed to tell me,

"I **am** fat."

"I **am** stupid."

"I **do** feel that God does not love me."

They firmly believe that no good thing can ever result from those facts, so I tell them...

"Learn to make a distinction between a fact, and what conclusions you draw from that fact."

For example, it may be absolutely true (a fact) that you are fat, but what you say internally (the conclusion) about your fatness determines whether you live a destructive or a productive life. Some of the **ungodly conclusions** about being fat include:

"I am fat (fact) so people don't like me (conclusion). They find me repulsive (conclusion)."

"I am fat (fact) so people think I am lazy (conclusion) and eat too much (conclusion)."

"I am fat (fact), and I'm not very sexy to my spouse (conclusion). The best thing I can do is try to avoid sex (conclusion)."

Some **godly conclusions** that can be drawn about being fat might include:

"Yes, I am fat (fact), but my spouse loves me anyway (godly conclusion), just the way I am (godly conclusion)."

"Yes, I am fat (fact), but thankfully it is not a permanent condition (godly conclusion). I am working each day on trying to bring my body back into submission (godly conclusion)."

"Yes, I am fat (fact), but I still have real value to God (godly conclusion), and to others in my circle of influence (godly conclusion), regardless of my weight."

"Yes, I am fat (fact), but that does not stop me from working in a productive ministry (godly conclusion)."

The fact that you are fat or thin, tall or short, young or old, does not produce ungodly self-talk.

The **ungodly conclusions** you make about your **tallness, fatness or age** determine your **destructive destiny!**

Godly conclusions produce a productive, happy life.

DISTORTED SELF-CONDEMNATION

Women and men frequently condemn themselves, even when they are actually doing good things. For example, it is common for a person to tell me, "Karen, I'm a very lazy person."

"Tell me something about your day," I respond. "What do you do in the morning?"

If the person is a housewife, she might answer, "I prepare breakfast for my children, then get them dressed and off to school. After they go to school, I do a little housework."

"What kind of housework do you do?" I persist.

"Well, I don't do the whole house everyday, but I do vacuum and make the beds."

"How about the laundry?"

"Yeah, I always do a couple of loads a day."

"Do you prepare an evening meal?"

"Well, yes, after I finish picking up the kids from school."

At that point, the lie of their laziness starts to be exposed.

"Well, I've got to tell you, that doesn't sound like a very lazy person to me."

Now, one word of caution here: as you read this little scenario, if your answer to my questions was "nothing", then laziness could be a problem to honestly address in your life! If it is, the next question you should ask yourself is, "What is a godly response to my laziness problem?"

You might answer, "Yes, it is true I am lazy, but I am taking steps to correct it. Today, I am going to do one positive thing in my home...I am going to vacuum the room that is most desperately in need of cleaning, whether I feel like doing it or not."

The fact is, you are lazy, but it is the conclusions and decisions you make concerning your laziness that will determine whether you lead a destructive or a productive life.

# CHAPTER NINE

My Private Hell!

In most of the healing workshops I have taught, in partnership with my friend, Margo Kreger, these last fifteen years, I have felt like a strong, powerful woman of God...except for one workshop!

In the midst of my normal strength and confidence, there was one workshop in particular where I had to fight a steady undercurrent of self-doubt. When I was not teaching the classes, I felt quite strong in other areas of ministry, counseling and reaching out to my friends. When Mike and I taught our Marriage God's Way classes together, there was a ministry anointing on us as a team, and I normally did not feel any adverse, individual attacks.

But, as the time drew near for the start of this particular healing workshop (I gave them twice a year, eight weeks each time), I began to feel an increasing pressure, a steady voice in my spirit that whispered, "You are going to be a miserable teacher this class. You have no compassion or concern for these women. Thank God you have Margo in the class to show these ladies that someone does care about them."

I knew I had to resist these feelings; I even knew they were not true. I would sometimes respond out loud, "No, I am not going to be miserable! God has given me this ministry, and He has prepared and gifted me to do it. I do care about these women. I've been doing this through the Holy Spirit for years, and lots of women have been mightily helped by God, so why should this next class be any different? Why should it be a disaster?"

Yet, as the class drew nearer, the attacks continued.

"Here comes the class, and you are not capable. You are weak, and not the right person to teach it. In fact, God has just brought in this new lady to help and train so you can be dismissed and drop out of sight. She felt such a 'burden' to come into your class because you are not what God wanted. You have no gifting. You fake it through every class. And, you really don't care about the women."

Imagine. I allowed this poisonous garbage to infiltrate and attack my mind, even after years of teaching the workshop!

The lies continued to bombard and sadden my spirit.

"Margo has the compassion. The giftings. Margo and this new lady will be the 'right' combination. It is obvious where their giftings are, and what God has given them for this class. But what has He given you?"

Do you see it? If left unchecked and unchallenged, ungodly self-talk becomes a persistent, merciless enemy, determined to devastate and devour (1 Peter 5:8).

As these destructive thoughts persisted, I still did not recognize that innocent baby who was voicing "truths" such as "You are not qualified," as a voice of the enemy with horns and a tail. Because I continued to give him room to attack, believing his lies, they were destroying my ability to live the fruitful life God had planned for me.

In my case, this ungodly self-talk started slowly, many months before the start of my class. Every now and then, to fight it, I'd pray a pleading prayer, trying to speak out positive talk, attempting to think good thoughts, but for some reason, the exercise bore little productive results; I became more intimidated as the class grew nearer.

MY PRIVATE HELL

I tried to act strong when I really felt weak.

In my mind, my inability to defeat the lies made me a hypocrite, and was another "truth" that proved I was not really qualified to teach the class.

When the class started, I felt the pressure increase. "Yes, it is true, Margo and Beth [not her real name] are my 'anointed' replacements."

The class felt like slow death.

In my mind, God was clearly showing me that Beth was placed in the class to handle the "difficult situations" through her discernment, anointing and giftings (all areas which I now firmly believed I was lacking).

Every lady who enrolled in the class was put through what I called a "2 on 1"...Margo and I [2] would pray individually over the person [1]. Normally, these prayer sessions lasted about three hours. During these times, I would ask each lady intimate questions about their past abuse, then lead them in prayers of forgiveness, healing and deliverance.

As the unchecked, ungodly self-talk became deeply rooted in my spirit, my prayers became less powerful; at the end of this continuing struggle, my prayers seemed absolutely futile. The harder I tried to pray and seek God, the more useless I felt.

84

I had given up.

I would look hopefully to Margo during these 2 on 1 sessions to rescue me from my powerless prayers, but she did not seem to discern the torment going on inside of me.

So nobody knew; it was my own, private hell.

I'd look at Margo and say, "Margo, why don't you lead this prayer today?", or "Margo, why don't you do the deliverance prayer?", or "Margo, would you please close in prayer?"

I spiritually shut myself out of God's process, convinced my participation would add more harm than good. Even though it was not obvious to Margo what I was doing, it was to me (Of course, I believed it was also obvious to everyone else.).

Suddenly, I felt embarrassed to be called "the leader" of this ministry; it was such a relief when this particular eight-week workshop was over!

But the relief did not last very long.

MY RELUCTANT CONFESSION

In just four short weeks, Mike and I were scheduled to teach a three-day Marriage Retreat. In my current pathetic spiritual condition, how could I possibly teach the wives anything? You need to believe in what you teach, and at that moment, I was failing "Self-talk 101."

One morning, as I reluctantly climbed out of bed to start the day, knowing I was another day closer to the retreat, the pain inside seemed unbearable. Michael was not aware of the internal struggle going on inside of me; I hadn't said a word to him or anybody else about it.

On this particular morning I closed the bedroom door, got down on my knees alongside of my bed, and cried out to God,

> "Lord, please help me. I can't do this retreat...not like this. You've taught me so much, and I don't want to throw it all away. Please God, help me. I just can't seem to help myself. Amen."

Feeling like a little girl pleading to her Daddy, I wiped away my tears, got up and opened the door, making my way down the hall and stairs to where Michael was standing in the kitchen. Before the thought even came into my head, the Holy Spirit poured these words out of my mouth: "Michael, I've got to talk to you."

"Okay, honey."

"First, you must understand, I don't want you to get mad at me, or to tell me that I should know better. Don't scold me, or act surprised that I have some-how let you down. That hurts me more. What I need from you right now is comfort, understanding, strength...and your prayers."

Mike's face looked really inquisitive.

"Okay, Karen, I promise I won't get mad. I'll be understanding no matter what you tell me. I promise. Now, what the heck is going on?"

Slowly, and embarrassingly, I shared with Mike how I'd been eaten alive by ungodly self-talk, and that it had been going on for three months. "Because I've let it go on for so long, I'm just too weak to do anything for myself to break out of it. Please help me."

Mike reached out to me, pulled me in close and hugged me saying, "Honey, I'm sorry that you are hurting."

I started to cry in my favorite safe place, Michael's arms. After I was done smearing and wetting his shirt, he took me by the hand and said, "Karen, let's pray and take spiritual dominion over this attack."

I looked at him and said, "You understand, Michael, at this point I can't muster up the strength. You've got to do all the praying."

"I understand."

Michael then began to take spiritual dominion over the enemy. He commanded the fear to leave (2 Timothy 1:7), and prayed for God's peace, power and strength to replace it. When he finished the prayer, he shared something the Holy Spirit had shown him.

"Honey, throughout the rest of this day, I believe the Holy Spirit wants you to declare, out loud, these words: 'I'm a powerful woman of God. I'm a powerful woman of God.' Do it all day long, out loud, at the top of your voice."

And I did.

At first I did not feel like a powerful woman of God, but the more times I declared that biblical truth (Hebrews 4:12) out loud, the more I began to notice increasing strength. The next day I was still declaring it.

When the marriage retreat finally started, God empowered me to give one of my very best testimonies ever! I shared my recent failures (the very story I'm sharing here now). It was my hard-learned, practical gift to them.

After three months in my private hell, the spiritual benefits from this destructive experience were deeply imbedded because it was so painful for so long. I had almost given up the ministry God gave to me; I was also ready to flee from ministry altogether, including the marriage classes and retreats. From that personal experience, I never ever wanted to fall into that place again where I was so defeated, so down that I would be willing to give up the ministries I so dearly loved, and felt so privileged to share with others.

CHAPTER TEN

Recognize, Rebuke, Replace

After the prayer time with Mike, I felt compelled to confess my weaknesses and failures to Margo, apologizing to her for my giving up, and for not asking for her help. It was important for me to be real, and to acknowledge how vicious these attacks can become to anyone, even teachers and leaders.

Walking in godly self-talk is a process; we never fully arrive.

Margo was loving and forgiving when I shared with her, but one of the things she said particularly hit me hard: "Karen, I couldn't tell. I am sorry you went through what you did, but I honestly was not aware of your pain. I'm so sorry that I did not have the opportunity to help you."

If you are currently entertaining ungodly self-talk, do not wait for a deep emotional experience to break this destructive behavior. The plan God has in place to protect you against attacks, and to break any current attacks, is as easy as one, two, three. I call it "God's Protection Plan" – **the three R's** of godly self-talk.

GOD'S PROTECTION PLAN

Step One: **R**ecognize the ungodly thought.

Step Two: **R**ebuke it. "That's not true."

Step Three: **R**eplace the lie with godly self-talk.

STEP ONE:
<u>RECOGNIZE</u> THE UNGODLY THOUGHT.

Even a young child can be trained to do this.

Learn to recognize the tiniest, subtle put-downs or lies about yourself, no matter how innocent or legitimate those thoughts or words might feel at the moment. Recognize that accepting the lies is the first step in your process to self-degradation, destruction and death.

Recognize the need to expose the lie.

These subtle put-downs become your belief system of who you are. That's why it is so important to catch them in the beginning, when they have no real strength. If you do as I did, and allow your mind to wallow in them for months (in some cases, years!), they start to take on a power and strength all their own.

Recognize them immediately!

Don't buy the lie!

Ask the help of the Holy Spirit to show you when you are focusing, concentrating and meditating on ungodly thoughts that match your feelings, or produce new, negative ones. The repeating of the ungodly thought gives it power. To stop giving the lie power, you must RECOGNIZE the lie and stop it.

When you start to feel depressed, down, "low" or ineffective, ask yourself, "What am I telling myself?" That is a good early indicator that will help you recognize the lie quickly.

One technique I use in my workshops to help others recognize the frequency of their ungodly self-talk is to have each member wear a rubber band on their wrist for a week. Each time they recognize an ungodly message in their mind, they are to snap the rubber band – hard. Within a few days, some are sporting rather prominent red welts on their wrists as a testimony to the power of ungodly self- talk in their lives. By the end of the week, most of the welts are gone and only a bit of redness remains.

STEP TWO:
<u>REBUKE</u> IT. "THAT'S NOT TRUE."

Today, the very first time I recognize something in my mind that is not uplifting, I immediately and aggressively attack it.

"No – that's not true!" I declare. "I do not buy the lie."

These negative thoughts burned me badly the last time I allowed them to invade my mind; I was miserable for three months. Now, I am determined not to go there again. I am extra cautious whenever the first sign of a subtle putdown emerges in my mind.

The reason it is so difficult to stop the negative thoughts is that you believe them. They have shaped you and been a part of you for so long that to try to change and replace them with a good thought is very difficult. The good thought is the one that "feels foreign" to you and seems like the lie.

For instance, all my life I believed I would never accomplish much because I was "not smart". My weak grades in school, combined with my poor testing, were "the proof" that I was not smart. I believed there was little I could do in any kind of profession except perhaps become a simple store clerk.

I fought that feeling and tried to get into nursing school, but failed the test. By then, I had accumulated all "the proof" I needed. Even when I tried and worked very hard, it made no difference...I was too dumb to do anything very challenging. My "truth", my conclusion for living was that "I am not smart. I do not have the abilities of those around me. Therefore, I will never accomplish much of anything in life."

The fact was true...I am not blessed with a brilliant mind. However, my conclusion that "Therefore, I cannot be used by God for anything" was incorrect.

STEP THREE: <u>REPLACE</u> THE LIE WITH GODLY SELF-TALK.

When I fight bad thoughts about myself, the difficult thing is to be able to override the past "proof" of my identity I've so passionately held onto all these years. I believed the false "truth": "I am incapable of producing anything good or worthwhile. I'm dumb!"

But to move into what God wanted for my life, I had to learn to reject the negative thought, and all the past "proof" I had that I was not smart, and somehow REPLACE those thoughts with a godly perspective. I started to declare this "killer statement" which brought death to the lies:

"Yes, it is true that I do not have the ability to do higher math, nor do I have the book learning capability that some other people have. There are many around me who can learn from books much easier than I can, but I am still teachable! Plus, God has given me His wisdom and His spiritual growth – those gifts have enriched my life, and the lives of others."

It is important for you to understand the value of obedience over feelings. I obeyed God's Word as shared in Philippians 4:8-9 by dwelling on godly thoughts, even if I did not "feel" they were true.

As you obediently declare His Word, transformation will begin to take place in your spirit. To begin to see yourself in a godly way, in line with God's Word, takes a consistent, obedient effort on your part to rebuke negative thoughts and replace them with godly ones. This process unleashes new ambitions and desires you may have never experienced before. By being obedient, God will begin to open up new doors as you destroy the negative world you currently live in and allow God to replace it with His vision for your life.

CHAPTER ELEVEN

No More Coattails

Before I started this journey, I fervently believed my fate in life was to ride on the coattails of my husband's success. After all, he was the bright one, the ambitious one, the one with the mandate from God to write Christian books and establish a Christian publishing company. My job was simply to support him; after all, "I'm not the smart one."

What I soon discovered was that when I began letting go of that old, dumb person, and started thinking godly thoughts such as "I am teachable," and "I am smart in some areas," God began to use me to bless others. I began to understand that I had a different kind of smarts...a biblical wisdom that comes from reading God's Word. The more I replaced ungodly thoughts with thoughts that lined up with God's Word, the less I could continue to call myself stupid.

I started to say...

"It's not true that I am stupid; I can learn; I am teachable, and God does teach and use me. He has a plan for my life, and His desire is to prosper me."

You must be willing to obey and speak out the new, godly thoughts about yourself, even if they do not initially feel right, even if you must force into your mind what feels like a lie, what feels like what you'd like to be, but you are not. Eventually, as you practice this biblical process, more and more good thoughts will be stored up in the front part of your mind, easy to grab onto, and all the past lies will be pushed back a little further. The more good stuff you put up in front, the more your mind will grab onto the latest input of your real truth.

Be satisfied with knowing that the change you "feel" will come later after many repetitions of the godly truths. Within a couple of days, if you are catching every negative thought, your spirit will start to be lifted as you journey on the exciting road that will change that old, destructive identity into a strong, powerful one that lines up with how God views you.

Is This Positive Thinking?

As I teach on this subject, someone will always ask, "Karen, isn't this just the same as what the world calls 'positive thinking'?"

Yes, it is positive thinking...but with an important distinction.

God tells us to be positive in our thoughts:

Finally, brethren, whatsoever things are true, whatsoever things are honest, whatsoever things are just, whatsoever things are pure, whatsoever things are lovely, whatsoever things are of good report; if there be any virtue, and if there be any praise, think on these things.

Those things, which ye have both learned, and received, and heard, and seen in me, do: and the God of peace shall be with you.

(Philippians 4:8-9)

God also instructs us to bring into "captivity" every thought:

...bringing into captivity every thought to the obedience of Christ.

(2 Corinthians 10:5)

Obviously, we want to be obedient to what God's Word says, and be receptive to whom He says we are.

The number one criteria in a godly thought is that it not just be positive, but that it line up with God's Word, with His vision for your life! That's why I prefer to call them "godly

thoughts" rather than "positive thoughts". Your thoughts must accurately reflect God's heart, and how He views you.

To achieve that goal, you must meditate on His Word (Psalm 118:148) and His godly view of you not because you are trying to "fool" or "trick" yourself into feeling good, but because you are trying to re-align yourself back to a position that reflects God's heart for you. You are retraining your thoughts and your mouth to speak those things that accurately reflect how God sees you.

A LOVE LETTER FROM GOD

In one of my classes a few years ago, a lady shared with us a letter entitled "My Beloved Child" which contained a series of Scriptures rearranged in the form of a love letter (Unfortunately, I do not know who to credit for compiling this series of Scriptures. If you know the compiler, let me know and I'll credit that person in the next edition of this book.). This powerful document has dramatically impacted many lives since it reveals, Scripture by Scripture, God's heart.

His standard is so much higher than our own.

His love is so much greater than we can imagine.

I pray this Scriptural love letter will help you think godly (positive) thoughts which are in line with His

Word! These Scriptures will help you see yourself the way He sees you – as a most precious and beloved person.

I'd strongly suggest that you read this love letter at least once each day out loud, allowing God's heart to sink deep into your spirit.

It is time to stand on and believe God's Word rather than your current lies. You may not believe you are capable, good or valuable, but you can declare positive, powerful, hopeful things because God's Word declares it for you! He has made you in a marvelous, unique way. You can indeed do all things because He has given you the traits, characteristics, ambitions and abilities to do it!

MY BELOVED CHILD

I have loved you with an everlasting love, with loving kindness and draw you to Me (Jeremiah 31:3). This love cannot be compared to any other love you have ever experienced or desired. My love for you is so deep it compelled Me to give My life for you on the cross (Hebrews 12:2). I cannot bear to have you stand afar from Me.

There is nothing that can separate you from My love (Romans 8:38-39). When everyone else deserts you and you feel all alone, I will never leave you or forsake you (Hebrews 13:5). When you are sad and crying, I am there to catch all of your tears. I save them in a bottle (Psalm 56:8). I promise to comfort you, and it is I who turn your tears into joy (Jeremiah 31:13). Unlike others who hold the past against you, I blot it out, remembering it no more (Isaiah 43:25).

I gaze at you through the Lattice (Song of Solomon 2:9), as My love compels Me to understand your every thought and word, and to know all your ways (Psalm 139:2-4). I know the number of hairs on your head (Matthew 10:30). I have carved an image of you on my hand (Isaiah 49:16), and My thoughts of you are more than the grains of sand (Psalm 139:18).

You are the apple of My eye (Deuteronomy 32:10).

My darling, don't forget about our covenant when you became Mine (Ezekiel 16:8), and I clothed you in fine linen and silk, and I adorned you with ornaments, putting bracelets on your wrists, a chain on your neck, a jewel in your nose, earrings in your ears, and a beautiful crown on your head. You are My child and you are perfected through My splendor (Ezekiel 16:10-14).

My dearest, I rejoice in the return of the love I have for you. I long for you to turn to Me with all your heart, all your mind, all your soul and strength (Matthew 22:37-38). I am knocking, just open the door (Revelation 3:20).

I rejoice when you trust in Me, and find that only in Me is satisfaction found (Psalm 37:3-7), and that with

Me there is a peace like no other (Philippians 4:7). Allow Me to give you the most thrilling plan existing, one better than you could ever imagine (Jeremiah 29:11).

I have given you a book describing the love I have for you. It will comfort you, and remind you of Me and My ways (Psalm 110). Meditate on it day and night (Psalm 1:2). Even though you do not see Me, believe in Me and you will rejoice with joy inexpressible until I come back for you (1 Peter 1:8).

I have gone to prepare a place for you. I'll be back soon.

Your Beloved Friend,
Jesus

CHAPTER TWELVE

Tanner's Awesome Lesson

As you begin to soak your spirit in the Word of God, you will find yourself declaring it to others, even when you did not intend to (as the following story illustrates).

One day I was driving home with all three of my grandkids in the back seat of my car: Tanner, 10, Austin, 10, and Valerie 8. As I was driving, they were causing a great deal of commotion; Tanner, in particular, was acting extra perky.

"Calm down so I can concentrate on my driving," I instructed them. After spending two hours on a hot summer morning with them and my sister, who was teaching my grandchildren how to ride her two horses, it did not seem like an unreasonable request. It was even more important since I was driving down a hill with winding roads. I was already dusty, dirty and tired. At this particular moment, their usually enjoyable noises became a distraction to my driving.

But the grandkids had no such concerns. I could tell from Tanner's voice that he was, on this particular day, the instigator of the screaming and yelling. Tanner was having a good time with the other two who were being inspired by his antics to add some mischief of their own.

"Tanner, calm down and be quiet, please. Grandma needs to concentrate so I can drive safely on these dangerous roads."

Their incessant noise made me tense, and I was becoming increasingly angry because they were not listening to me. For the next thirty seconds the chaos in the back seat grew even louder. As the volume increased, my patience shortened. Finally, I needed to make a firm statement so I pulled the car off to the side of the road and stopped.

The kids, being my brilliant grandkids, instinctively knew something was wrong.

In my mind, I had intended to tell Tanner how disobedient he'd been to his Grandma, and that I needed his help to have quiet and calmness in the car. Instead, when I turned around and looked right at Tanner, ready to release a mouth full of stern, rebuking words, with my body full of tenseness and aggravation, I blurted out, "Tanner, do you know what you are?"

He looked at me surprised and quiet, his eyes open wide, very attentive. I had his attention. After a few second pause, something unexpected, even shocking, came out of my mouth.

"You are awesome!"

Tanner looked very relieved and surprised. He released a big smile from ear to ear, but not a word came out of his mouth.

Stunned at what had come out of my own mouth, all I could do was slowly turn around like I actually understood what had just happened, and started the car. As I pulled back onto the road, my mind was filled with thoughts like...

"Wow. What just happened? I know that was You, Lord, because those weren't my words. That wasn't my plan. What are You trying to show me? What do You want me to learn from this?"

The rest of the car ride home was quite pleasant; the grandkids were calm and well-behaved.

As I thought and meditated on what had happened so suddenly that it had actually stunned me, I began to understand that the day was a learning experience for Tanner and for Grandma. God had shown me once again that a compliment will always produce far more fruit than criticism. In this case, the Holy Spirit took control of my tongue and caused me to speak God's love when I wanted to speak out something else.

That's why I encourage you to read the love letter in the last chapter many times over until it becomes part of who you are. It will instill in your spirit how much God loves you; as a result, you will begin to speak God's love to others. And, as you read God's Word, pay particular attention to those Scriptures that describe His heart toward you.

Reading God's Word will prepare you for everyday situations such as I experienced with my grandkids, and it will also fortify you when the enemy tries to convince you that you do not have the ability to complete the next challenge God gives you.

In the face of the devil's deceptions, you can confidently reply:

> *And my God shall supply all your [my] need according to his riches in glory by Christ Jesus.*
> (Philippians 4:19)

CHAPTER THIRTEEN

Choice Versus Results

God blessed me with three children, and like most mothers, my desire has always been to serve and teach them. As they grew up, I believe I was fairly effective at accomplishing that goal. And, when raising my kids got a bit rocky, I'd confidently reassure myself, "Karen, you are a good mom. This was just a little setback. No biggie."

Yes, there were times I was lazy.

Yes, at times I said things I shouldn't have said. But through my twenty-five years of raising children, I hope and pray my kids would say today, "Overall, our Mom did a pretty good job."

Being a mom was the best part of my life! I believed motherhood was "the most important profession" because, as a mother, I was given the joy and privilege of molding three children's lives.

As I look back on that time, I am forever grateful that the mothering part of my life was seldom hampered by ungodly thoughts such as, "What an awful mother I am," or "That was a bad thing I did to them," or "I'm such an awful mother that my children are going to grow up to be hoodlums." Motherhood was one area where I had strong confidence and good training; I emulated my own dear mother, Katherine DeCarlo, who raised all seven of her daughters in godly values.

With God's grace, most of the time I thought, "Whatever they decide to become is up to them. My job is to give them a strong supportive foundation, based on godly values."

Like most other moms, I sacrificed for my children, and did about everything I could for their benefit. I knew and <u>believed</u> that I was a good mom, seldom second-guessing my ability in that area.

THE QUESTIONING MOTHER

Conversely, one of my friends was also a very good mom, probably a better mom than I was (judging by the things she told me she did for her kids). Yet, to this day she still suffers from the nagging anxiety that "I was not a good enough mother to my children"...even though she clearly went beyond what most mothers do.

Now her children are adults. Yet, each time they make a mistake, or go through a hard time, my friend still takes on personal responsibility, declaring, "I must have done something wrong." She blames everything that goes wrong in their adult lives on her supposed failures as a mother. I can't tell you how many times I've told her, "I was a great mom, but you were better. You always went that extra mile for your kids."

To this day, this lady still suffers incredible guilt and condemnation when her children struggle, even to the point of becoming ill, locking herself in her home, or hiding from others because she feels so badly about herself as a mom.

YOUR CHOICE!

Two different perspectives...two different choices – that hopefully demonstrate the difference between deciding to live in joy by practicing godly self-talk, versus deciding not to enjoy life and suffer – based on the choice to accept or reject God's Word in our lives.

Whatever station of life you are in, be it as a mother, a pastor, a politician or a poet, these godly decisions will determine how your life unfolds, and how you impact those around you.

111

CHAPTER FOURTEEN

Walking in the Middle
of a Very Tiny Stream

One of my sons had some particularly difficult struggles in his young life. My husband and I tried to help in whatever he was going through, but without much success. We knew he was unhappy, but we didn't know why. When the time came for him to get married to a very sweet, sensitive young lady, Mike and I were happy for him, and hoped he would now begin to reap some of the deeper joys of life.

After his marriage, there was still an off and on coldness to Mike and me; we simply did not know what was happening to him beneath the surface. At times he would decide to no longer speak to us. Of course, this was devastating, especially since we did not understand why. The pain was so deep that I was consumed with rejection. I knew I was a good mom, so I could not understand why one of my sons didn't view me as lovable.

Clearly, to survive, I needed a better approach to this sad situation.

My very close girlfriend, Margo, came to me one day and said that as she was praying for my son she saw our family reunited, having fun and praying together on the front lawn of our home. I took that as "my encouragement from God"—a vision to grasp and believe no matter what the current circumstances were like.

I accepted what Margo shared with me because we had a long spiritual history together; I trusted her prayer life. She is cautious and careful about what she shares, and with whom she shares it. Unless God speaks to her clearly, she won't say anything. Because she is such a godly woman, I received her words with 100% enthusiasm as a true word from God.

Now I could happily go on with my life knowing the end result was destined to be good. I told myself over and over, "Why be sad? Why be upset? God has promised a wonderful reunion with my son. God has shown me that our family will be reunited and we will enjoy each other's company once again!"

That vision enabled me, every single day, to embrace joy rather than sorrow, and that made a major difference in how I experienced each day.

I prayed for my son every day, and never held anything against him. Instead, I looked with great anticipation to the future, rejoicing in the ultimate great result for our family.

STREAM IN THE VALLEY

One morning I woke up feeling a bit blue, not because I was depressed, but because I missed my son. At church that morning the lady in front of me turned around and asked, "Can I pray for you?"

"Sure, please do," I replied.

I thought to myself, *"Lord, You are so good. I don't know why You take such good care of me, but thank You for loving me this morning."*

Looking back on it, I realize now that this lady had been praying for me quietly during the entire church service. At the same time, a lady in back of me tapped me on the shoulder and said, "I've been praying for you."

"Thank you, that feels good," I replied.

By the end of the service I realized I wasn't blue anymore.

Our church had a special healing service that night, and I went to help with the people who needed prayer. One lady who was also there to help pray came up to me and said, "Karen, God's put you on my heart; He wants me to pray for you." So, her and a couple of other ladies took me into the pastor's office and said, "We don't know why God wants this prayer for you, so we'll just pray quietly."

No words were spoken as these three women prayed over me for about two minutes. Then, the prayer was over.

"Karen, I've got a vision," one lady said. "You were in this deep, deep valley, and at the bottom of it was a little stream, not much of a stream, and you were walking right in the middle of it. Jesus was right in front of you. Do you know what that means?"

"I haven't a clue," I replied, thinking, *"Lord, what does this vision mean? I sure don't know. What are You trying to tell me? I really want to hear."*

And as I got up from the couch, the meaning of the vision came to me instantly.

"I know what it means."

"You said I was in this deep, deep valley. At the bottom of this deep valley there was a stream, and I was walking right in the middle of it. That stream is the promise God gave me for my son. I didn't even

116

know I was in a deep valley because of the promise. I have kept my eyes on the promise, so I am in a good place. It was a little stream and a little promise, but when God says anything, it is true."

The promise kept me out of depression because I refused to go to that place where it would bring me to anger, bitterness and loneliness, eating up my life.

How good God was to me that day when I felt a little blue from missing my son.

How lovingly He took care of this mother who had an ache in her heart.

How He confirmed that night the vision that Margo gave me for the future was truly God's Words, and more than ever, no matter how long the wait, I was encouraged to be patient and wait with a joyful heart.

It was my choice to embrace that promise or to throw it away (as though God said nothing). I am so glad that I chose to believe that God's promise was real. My mind was filled with thoughts about our reunion with my son. I saw him sitting at the dinner table with us, enjoying us, eating some of his "home cooked" favorites. I pictured us praying together, having fun together – because I chose to hold onto the promise.

At any moment, if I gave up that promise, I would become blue, and my mind could be filled with negative, angry thoughts.

My self-talk was all about the promise – a promise that preserved me through many years of potential devastation.

"I CAN BARELY STAND IT."

My joy rested in the vision, and I would frequently remind my husband, Mike, about it.

"Mike, there's no reason to be sad because our son will come back to us down the road. Why be sad now, when the outcome is so good?"

"Well, that's nice how you feel," Mike would reply, "but I just can't see it that way. To me, this is devastating. I can hardly bear it."

During the next couple of years, as Mike saw the joy in my attitude, he came to me one day and said, "Tell me about the vision again because I can't stand feeling the way I do anymore. It is tearing me apart inside."

As I shared the vision with extreme exuberance, my husband decided to *embrace the promise*. He clearly experienced relief as he looked right into my eyes and said, "Tell it to me again. I want to get it grounded deep in my spirit."

From that day on, we both held onto the promise, and our minds were focused on the outcome, not the current circumstances. This simple decision lifted my husband's spirit tremendously; he no longer was a depressed father longing for his son.

THE LONG WAIT

This relationship with our son of being "on again, off again" continued for years. Each time the relationship would start up, and we would begin to be hopeful, something would happen that would cause our son to withdraw again.

Still...the roller coaster ride of our relationship did not discourage us from keeping our focus on what God had already promised. Personally, I believed God gave Margo that vision to fortify us during the long time that would pass before our family healing finally came into fruition.

One day, our son called us, and his voice had a totally different tone. Although he was still cautious and a little bit apprehensive, he was clearly different. We once again started a new relationship, knowing only time would tell if this was the moment God was talking about.

It was!

We have enjoyed his caring, his loving, his generosity, his company and his sense of humor ever since. We now have a wonderful relationship, and our family times together are precious.

We plan on many more.

 # CHAPTER FIFTEEN

"Lord, I Know I'm Not Perfect, But Don't Tell My Husband."

One evening when we were counseling a young couple, Mike was explaining to them the importance of nurturing your spouse.

"It is important to learn how to ignore the faults of your spouse," he told them. "Concentrate only on acknowledging those things they do that are uplifting. Give up your right to be your spouse's critic! Refuse to assume the role of their parent. Instead, become their enthusiastic cheerleader."

Mike paused for a second to compose himself. He so badly wanted this young couple to absorb these life-changing principles that he could barely contain his passion. Then, he began again.

"You can literally change your spouse's life by what you choose to feed them. Uplifting, encouraging words will produce a strong, happy spirit in your spouse. Even if your spouse is not the wonderful person you want them to be just yet, through your good words and actions, they will begin to change. Remind them of every good thing that they are and do. Your constant, steady stream of affirming words will gradually help transform your spouse into a joyful, productive person who feels deeply loved."

As I was listening to Mike share, God revealed to me how well Mike had been doing just that very type of nurturing in our own marriage during the last twenty plus years! Mike had literally helped me change my perspective through a flood of constant compliments and assurances. He created a climate that enabled me to feel secure as his wife, and as a mother to our children. I actually had been so conditioned by Mike's godly words over the years that I actually believed, "He doesn't think I have any faults."

At that moment I had to interrupt him.

"Mike, I want to share with them, and with you, how the wonderful, good words which you have so freely poured on me have made me feel like I have no faults at all. Oh, I know I do, but you have made me feel that in your eyes I am perfect."

It was hard for me to explain this to the young couple.

I could verbalize, "Oh, yes, I know I have faults," but there was no emotion to go with that statement because Mike had literally brainwashed (soul-washed?) me into thinking that I was <u>his</u> perfect woman!

Now, this is particularly a God-given miracle when you understand that in our Marriage God's Way class I described the first thirteen years of our marriage as "hell"! Those early years (I can say "early" since we've been married 42 years as of this writing) were filled with Mike's put-downs and complaints.

"You don't hug enough."

"You don't kiss enough."

"You are too tough on the kids with your discipline."

On and on.

Mike was totally unhappy with me, and focused firmly on my faults.

Yet, here I was in the living room that night sharing, "Oh, I know I have faults, but deep down in my spirit I honestly can't think of any."

I thought to myself, *I know I'm not perfect*, but it was hard to say, not because I am full of my own self-importance or perfection, but because Mike had been so convincing over the last three decades that he had made me believe I <u>was</u> *his* "perfect woman" (his term, not mine). Mike also openly calls me his "total woman" in front of our family and friends. When a wife is called the "total woman" by her husband for a few decades, she begins to believe her husband really means it!

THE BOOMERANG EFFECT

The other impact of Mike's love fest on me was that I could not help but search for ways to give compliments back to this nourishing husband of mine. As a result, compliments and encouraging words have so permeated our marriage that they have become a normal, daily part of our lives. Mike gives a compliment to me and I boomerang one right back to him.

We see our primary role with each other as CHEERLEADER, and have learned to bring every ungodly, negative thought "into captivity" according to 2 Corinthians 10:5. God's Word tells us to choose life and blessing in our own lives, in our marriages, and in our relationship with others. As we do, our lives become fruitful and productive.

> *...I have set before you life and death, blessing and curses. Now choose life, so that you and your children may live.*
>
> (Deuteronomy 30:19-20)

124

There's a little poem Mike and I use in our Marriage God's Way class that emphasizes, in a simple way, how this principle of life and death choices works in nature, and can be applied symbolically to our own lives.

HUMMINGBIRDS FOR LIFE!

Both the hummingbird and the vulture fly over our nation's deserts.

All vultures see is rotting meat, because that is what they look for. They thrive on that diet.

But hummingbirds ignore the smelly flesh of dead animals. Instead, they look for the colorful blossoms of desert plants.

The vultures live on what was. They live on the past. They fill themselves with what is dead and gone.

But hummingbirds live on what is. They seek new life. They fill themselves with freshness and life.

Each bird finds what it is looking for. We all do.

Quote Magazine; (Author Unknown)

Do you see yourself as a vulture or a hummingbird? How do you think others such as your friends, your children, or your spouse see you?

If you are a vulture now, you are not stuck! Begin to apply godly self-talk to your life. As you do, God's principles will literally transform you from a vulture to a hummingbird!

Charles Swindoll grasped the significance of a godly mentality when he wrote this powerful little piece on attitudes (shared with permission).

ATTITUDES
By Charles Swindoll

The longer I live, the more I realize the impact of attitude on life. Attitude, to me, is more important than facts.

It is more important than the past, than education, than money, than circumstances, than failures, than successes, than what other people think or say or do.

It is more important than appearance, giftedness, or skill. It will make or break a company...a church...a home...a person.

The remarkable thing is we have a choice every day regarding the attitude we will embrace for that day. We cannot change our past...we cannot change the fact that people will act in a certain way. We cannot change the inevitable. The only thing we can do is play on the one string we have, and that is our attitude.

I am convinced that life is 10% what happens to me and 90% how I react to it. And so it is with you...we are in charge of our attitudes.

START KICKIN' AND DON'T STOP

Even as I have been writing this book, I have had to fight ungodly self-talk. Some of my thoughts have been...

"I have nothing that big to share."

"This book is not that important to anybody else."

"I'm sure people have heard all of this before."

"This is no big deal."

That's my ungodly self-talk. As soon as I recognize it, I calmly fight it in my head by replacing it with things such as...

"You are not going to go there."

"Anything God generates is a big deal."

"I will not minimize this."

"God is wise enough to know how He wants to use this book to reach and touch others."

Many of you right now have a very big boulder in the road of your life called "ungodly self-talk". That boulder stops you from going forward. It looms as something far too large for you to remove. But you can remove that boulder, you can destroy it through God's help and biblical principles.

I pray that you will decide to choose godly self-talk to destroy that boulder and clear the road for the rest of your life as you apply His life-changing truths.

Godly self-talk brings freedom; ungodly self-talk condemns.

You have the power to decide whether you receive freedom or condemnation. You can say, "There's nothing I can do" and continue to suck up all the seeds of death, or you can say, "I decide to choose life."

Our thought life is a daily process that we monitor, minute-by-minute.

I pray you will start to *Kick the Baby Off the Cliff* in your own life today. Remember, ungodly self-talk looks innocent, but it's not. Don't buy the lie! Kick every single one of those ungodly lies out of your life.

And please, once you start kickin', don't stop.

NOTE PAGES

Is God Leading You to Write or Publish a Book?

If so, CSN can help.

Since 1984, Christian Services Network (CSN) has served pastors, teachers, counselors and lay leaders around the world!

CSN specializes in helping pastors and other Christians publish their books, or transform their taped sermons into bookstore quality books. Our family of clients have sold millions of books!

CSN helps you create or book, or take a book you've created and perform any service you need, including: proofing, editing, typesetting, cover design, publishing, promotion, marketing and distribution.

CSN is your "Partnership Publisher". We produce your "bookstore quality" book, and unlike most publishers, you keep the profits! If you are 1) a first time author, or 2) an experienced author who wants to reach out beyond your own city, CSN can help sell your book. CSN bookstore buyers are constantly seeking new teaching, inspirational and counseling materials.

For more information, call us toll free at 1-866-484-6184, or write us at:

CSN Books
1975 Janich Ranch Court
El Cajon, CA 92019-1150

THE ORDER PAGE

To order additional copies of **Kick the Baby Off the Cliff** please fill out the order form below and send it to us along with a check payable to:

CSN
1975 Janich Ranch Ct.
El Cajon, CA 92019

Or you may call our toll free order line at: 1-866-484-6184, or order online at: www.CSNbooks.com/Wourms

Kick the Baby Off the Cliff

Please rush me_____book(s) at $14.95 each.	$_____
I am enclosing $2.95 shipping and handling per book. _____**book(s) x $2.95 each =**	$_____
Total enclosed:	$_____